W9-CFI-786

Living

with a...

GAMER

Charlie Mills

with Daniel Kleinman

Living

with a...

GAMER

Charlie Mills

with Daniel Kleinman

Red Rock Press   New York

To my eternally patient parents—Charlie Mills

Red Rock Press   New York, New York
www.RedRockPress.com

ISBN 9781933176-26-0

Library of Congress Cataloging-in-Publication Data

Mills, Charlie.
  Living with— a gamer / by Charlie Mills.
      p. cm.
  ISBN 978-1-933176-26-0
 1. Parenting—Humor. 2. Video games and children. 3. Video
gamers—Humor. 4. Video gamers—Psychology. I. Title.
  PN6231.P2M55 2008
  818'.602--dc22

                          2008043519

American Editor: Daniel Kleinman
Illustrations: Tom Hughes
Senior Editor: Kate Parker
Design: Zoe Mellors
Editorial Direction: Rosemary Wilkinson
Production: Melanie Dowland
Cover design: Zoe Mellors and Tom Hughes

Photo credit: p. 66 Rex Features

Printed in Malaysia

CONTENTS

WHAT IS GAMING?

And what has it done to this kid?

Do you remember when the TV was for watching Saturday morning 'toons, and the computer helped with schoolwork? Oh, the very notion is laughable now. Hilarious. You had visions of him or her watching life-enhancing documentaries or diligently sitting down at the computer to create a math-tastic spreadsheet, perhaps using the internet purely to reference a scholarly quote. Bless your sweet, naive socks.

Now, the computer is home to one thing only: games. What was once the television is now taken over by Xboxes, Playstations and something that is seriously called a Wii. Consoles and handhelds clutter every available surface and your house is filled with more wires than a nuclear reactor.

You are living with a Gamer.

So what's it all about? Put simply, he or she plays computer games for fun. In a gamer's mind, it is about honor and glory and battling on to the Next Level (capitals intended: it is a Big Deal). To you, the onlooker, the sight of this young person sitting hunched up in a dark room, with thumbs dancing a whirling dervish and pupils dilated with furious delight at the flashing screen seems a bit odd. Sinister, even.

You don't understand the appeal. Well, without wishing to damage your ego too much, this kid basically thinks gaming is more satisfying than a conversation with you. There—don't you feel better now it is out in the open? To make things absolutely high-definition clear: your function is purely to ensure the power is switched on at all times and to avoid moving your body between Gamer's face and the screen. Ever. Got that?

Your resident Gamer is obsessed with games, joyfully addicted to them. *Halo, Guitar Hero, Madden NFL* and *World of Warcraft* exert a much bigger hold on him than you do—probably bigger than anything a humble non-gamer like you can even imagine. Are you panicked yet?

But wait! Before you stage an intervention and pack him off to reform school / a remote desert with no electricity supply, read this book. You will learn to understand your Gamer, to know what makes him switch, seemingly instantly, from a dark mood to punching the air with unreserved joy and shouting, "In your face!" As you study these pages, your insight into his penchant for ignoring everything you say will grow and you will be able to translate his ever-growing techie vocabulary (w00t! pwned!) so you are "playing on the same level."

From there, you are in enough of a position of power to take the system down from the inside. Get Gamer back on your team, so to speak. Soon, you and your resident Gamer will be engaged in life-enriching conversations, skipping hand-in-hand in the sunshine and spending quality time together. You could get an occasional hug or a muffled, "I love you." Or, at least, you won't be totally ignored and moaned at. You might even hear the magic words, "Thank you," when not made in grateful reference to the purchase of a new game. What have you got to lose? Read on.

HOW TO SPOT A
Gamer

From the outside looking in, Gamer's behavior is quite baffling. Take a deep breath, exhale, then do this quiz to help you understand what you are dealing with...

		YES	NO
1	Is he openly plotting world domination?	❏	❏
2	Does he believe his prowess at *Grand Theft Auto* gives him the right to criticize your driving?	❏	❏
3	Has he lost sleep in order to make it to the Next Level?	❏	❏
4	If you were to confiscate the control mid-game and hold it for ransom, do you think he would fail to find your stunt amusing, then actually turn purple and explode like a meteorite from hell?	❏	❏
5	Do you often wonder if he has a rare genetic disorder that means he is genuinely deaf to your voice?	❏	❏

		YES	**NO**
6	Has it been an unearthly long time since he offered to do something useful around the house?	☐	☐
7	Is he seriously considering getting a catheter fitted so necessary bodily functions will not interrupt his Wii-Wii sessions?	☐	☐
8	If your house was burgled, is there a chance the thief would be unable to remove the gaming equipment from your house without Gamer leaving the building with him?	☐	☐
9	Does he seem largely unconcerned by your worries for his mental health?	☐	☐
10	If the President of the United States or LeBron James were to phone as he was zooming through the final level of *Halo*, would he yell, "Not now!"	☐	☐

If you answered YES to five or more of these, then congratulations! You are living with a Gamer.

BEING A GAMER:
The Rules

RULE 1

You don't need to "get a life"—you are a gamer: you have lots of lives.

RULE 2

Right trigger shoots, left trigger hurls grenades. Don't they teach you anything in school?

RULE 3

Learn to throw down your controller in frustration at a velocity that will show it who is boss, but not damage it irreparably. That little controller is like a direct line to heaven and without it you will cry sorry, sorry tears.

RULE 4

Referring to a member of your household as "Resident Evil" because they interrupted a game is amusing, granted, but not exactly kind. You are better than that.

RULE 5

If the cat insists on sitting in your lap while you play, one of you is going to end up clawing off the other's limb.

RULE 6

Just as the legendary Tom Jones is said to insure his chest hair for $7 million, you should take out insurance on your thumbs. They are the twin gods of leisure, and worth every penny.

RULE 7

Get a good game-face or no one will take you seriously. Furrow your brow, chew down on your lip and stare at the screen like your life depends on it. Because it does, in a way.

RULE 8

Come up with a creative and unique game name like "iambetterthanyouhaha" (and have a back-up ready just in case you lose the game in the first 30 seconds and feel too ashamed to go back for another beating).

RULE 9

You can get up and play over and over again when your onscreen body is riddled with bullets, but when your thumbs start to bleed and tremble from the console, it's time to take a break.

RULE 10

Create some of your own, seemingly anodyne curses to scream when you lose a game. Yelling, "Oh, you absolute *Flunkhead*!" is guaranteed to save you from a lot of trouble.

EVOLUTION OF A GAMER

Was your rosy-faced boy abducted by aliens who implanted him with the robot gene? No-your darling one's dark turn went a little something like this...

STAGE 1

He is not just "normal,"
he is a dream to live with:
always chatty, helpful and
considerate. He wows you
with sweet little questions
like, "Where do rainbows
come from?" and, "What's
the dog doing to the couch?"
and when he laughs
enthusiastically at your jokes
it makes you feel warm and
fuzzy inside. On Saturdays,
he likes to watch
"SpongeBob SquarePants"
and when the show is over
he turns off the television
and goes upstairs to play
with his action figures. Then
one day a friend ties him to
a chair and forces a computer
game upon him...

STAGE 2

The controls seem to be superglued to his hands, and when you finally wrench his fingers free, the game music continues to play in his head. He only has half an ear on what you are saying and for the first time in your life you wonder if you are boring (as if!–the very notion!). He is not interested in anything going on in the real world and has found refuge from his everyday life in the thrills of his new games. He appears genuinely baffled when the clock strikes midnight faster than he can say, "Just one more game."

STAGE 3

You are woken in the night by the commotion of him sleep-gaming as he dreams about aliens, firing grenades and dodging falling *Tetris* blocks. For the first time in living history, he wakes up early on Saturday and Sunday—to play more games, of course. It has become the "Wii-kend" now. Woe betides the fool who makes arrangements that interfere with this rigorous gaming schedule. Grandparents go unvisited and sports fields are abandoned. Unless you count *Madden* that is. The dented pads of his thumbs bear the mark of his dedication and his eyes are bloodshot with concentration.

STAGE 4

He tries to take the day off school because, man, he was so close. You wonder if you should give him the day off anyway because he looks ill—mentally, perhaps. When he is not hammering the console, he can be found posting on gaming forums. He then returns to the game, increasingly competitive and determined to wipe the floor with his new score. He has grown his hair long in order to thrash more effectively when playing *Guitar Hero*. From the elated shouts of "Pwned!" coming from his room, you gather that (a) "pwned" translates roughly to, "Hurrah, you are annihilated, I am victorious," and (b) shaggy, long hair helps.

STAGE 5

He worships blindly at the altar of computer games, eBaying everything that isn't nailed down in order to feed his habit. You notice that more people refer to him by his gaming name than his real name, although you can't quite bring yourself to call him "HotHulkHero." He believes that when he dies, a big "GAME OVER" will flash before his eyes. Despite being afraid to open the front door because of all the aliens and snipers lurking behind it, he manages to get a job that involves testing games and getting paid for it. And to rub salt into your disbelieving eyes, he gets paid a lot more than you. Pwned indeed.

LIVING WITH A GAMER:
DOs and DON'Ts

DOs

1   DO impose some sort of electric blackout every night, otherwise Gamer will play until his thumbs are numb and his eyes are bleeding.

2   DO swap the ready supply of Fritos he has next to the console for healthy carrot sticks, because he probably won't notice what he shoves in his mouth anyway.

3   DO test the above theory by replacing the carrot sticks with cat food. (But only do this if you are prepared for the inevitable inspection by Child Protection).

4   DO appeal to Gamer's competitive side by saying things like, "I bet you can't load the dishwasher in less than two minutes." It *might* work.

5   DO remind him that just because he has an impressive level of skill at *Mario Kart* and *Grand Theft Auto*, he is not allowed to drive your car.

6 DO allow yourself to dream that your Gamer might be
as intelligent as Stephen Hawking if only he applied
himself to theoretical physics instead of *Halo*.

7 DO download a ringtone that replicates the music
that only plays as you win *Pokemon*–he'll be totally
psyched out.

8 DO send in your pet to disturb him and slobber
enthusiastically over the console if you have lost the
nerve to enter his cordoned-off space yourself.

9 DO bear in mind that when he says, "I am saved," he
is referring to a technical aspect of the game and not
finding God or some other kind of spiritual redemption.
Still, it's an encouraging start.

10 DO feed his dinner to the cat if he isn't at the table in
the next half hour.

DON'Ts

1   DON'T bother telling him that playing computer games will rot his brain if you happen to be engrossed in "Deal or No Deal" at the time. It kinda loses your point.

2   DON'T be alarmed if you get woken at 7a.m. by heavy gunfire. It is unlikely to involve actual blood, just a lot of plasma screen.

3   DON'T think you are mature enough to stop yourself snickering when your gamer says, "I'm playing with my Wii." Yes, it is pronounced, "wee"—as in pee. Just imagine how many thousands of dollars worth of marketing genius thought that one up.

4   DON'T believe him when he says, "Just one last game." What kind of fool are you? Please.

5   DON'T let Gamer kid himself that playing *Madden NFL 09* will give him the body of Eli Manning. Only push-ups, pull-ups, weight lifting and running will help him achieve that goal.

6   DON'T expect him to recall anything that is not stored on a memory card.

7 DON'T be surprised if the game he is playing NEVER ends.

8 DON'T assume that when he says, "My name is Gamer and I am a computer game addict," he is not proud of himself. He is *bursting* with pride. If he were an avatar, he would actually explode in an eruption of white light.

9 DON'T underestimate how seriously your Gamer takes his hobby. He is probably campaigning to make "Gaming" a tax-exempt religion.

10 DON'T ask for a lesson unless abject humiliation is your thing.

INSIDE GAMER'S BEDROOM:
A Spotter's Guide

Yikes, be careful! Those cables you see trailing all over the carpet are worse than tripwires. This guide to Gamer's inviolate space lets you view it from a safe distance...

1   Curtains **Like those of Count Dracula, Gamer's drapes are always drawn. It is not that he is allergic to the sun (though it may go that way if he does not go outside sometime soon) but glare on the screen is his worst enemy. If Gamer is ever going to beat the game, the sun must be banished.**

2   Chair **This is no ordinary item of furniture: it is a special *gaming* chair. Everything is ergonomically designed to perfection. When Gamer sits in it, the console rests in his lap just so and his refreshing beverage is within arm's reach so he can sip it between levels without breaking concentration—much like a marathon runner at a water station.**

3   Wardrobe **A ghost town. There's no need for clothes when adventures are all computer-generated.**

4   Wires **What looks to you like a tangled maze of wires is in fact as carefully crafted as a bird's nest. Gamer can reach a hand in and pick out the "Wiimote" at a moment's notice. If you were to try the same move, you would get an electric shock like a taser stun to the power of 10. Hands off.**

5   Bookshelf **A quaint name for planks of wood that hold no books whatsoever, just cases upon cases of games. If that is not enough to signal the end of civilization as you know it, none of the games are in the correct box. Anyone with OCD, look away now.**

6   Door   **When you innocently pop your head around the door to offer fresh-baked cookies, Gamer automatically tries to move his crosshair on you. Duck.**

7   Dirty pile of unspecified items   **Half-eaten bags of chips and old pizza crusts are buried beneath sweat-stained T-shirts and smelly sneakers. Approach with caution and industrial-strength rubber gloves.**

8   Posters   **Other people decorate their bedrooms in such a way that might help them get a good night's sleep. Gamer doesn't go down that route: his walls are festooned with posters from *Devil May Cry* and *James Bond.* Feel free to redress the balance by blowing up a photograph of your fine self to A2 size and getting busy with the Blu-Tack. Why would he not be pleased with that!**

9   Discarded energy drink cans   **The secret to Gamer's success. Where lesser players have been killed off, your caffeine-charged champion fights into the night. If your sleep is being sacrificed as a result of Gamer's late-night energy, steal one of his drinks for the morning.**

10   Noodle-based ready meals   **Time spent at the dinner table is time wasted. Gamer needs food that is quick to make and can be poked into his body and sucked down without the effort of chewing. Call Rachel Ray quick.**

WHAT KIND OF GAMER IS HE?

Not all gamers are created equal...

THE CASUAL GAMER

The rare casual gamer is keen, but not yet willing to devote the necessary hours and days to practicing. He does not (yet) try to compete with his hardcore gamer friends or to wow you with tales of record-breaking scores. Mr. Casual is distracted by sunny days, phone calls and, on Sunday morning, teasing the cat with the smell of bacon. Soon though, casual gamers will see through your cunning plans to guide their attention elsewhere. You can't win. The call of the game is stronger than you. When a casual gamer begins to stockpile allowances to save up for a new console and library of games, you're done for.

THE HARDCORE GAMER

Often to be found debating the finer points of whether *FIFA Soccer 08* was better than *09*, Mr. Hardcore tries to convince you that gaming is a sign of highly intelligent life forms. The hardcore gamer has the commitment that the old-time day traders had before uncertainty rocked their world. Hardcore gamers cannot remember what a weekend felt like without a console in his hand. Yet there is a shred of hope. The merely hardcore gamer can be coaxed out of the player's pit occasionally, if only to beg you for more money to spend on games. You have a job reminding gamers in this advanced category that Luther Vandross and Janet Jackson could be right: the best things in life are free. Suggest that, and the gamer will look at you blankly for a nanosecond before turning back to the screen.

THE ÜBER GAMER

Über gamers are so dedicated that they allow their passion for this "sport" to override any semblance of social grace. If you elicit a grunt or sigh from an über gamer, think yourself über lucky. The über gamer doesn't need your friendship, sucker. Thanks to multiplayer online games, gamers have thousands of friends. The fact that the gamer you live with is never going to meet them in the flesh, makes you feel even more unpopular. How annoying. You are also in awe of Über Gamers' ambition: they excitedly anticipate the launch of a new game for six months straight, whereas you frequently get to the weekend and wonder what you are doing with your life. Über Gamer has clearly focused goals and is not afraid to game for 47 hours solid to reach them. Impressive, eh?

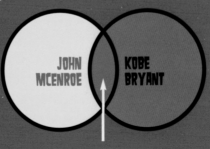

JOHN MCENROE

KOBE BRYANT

COMPETITIVE GAMER

GAMER VENN: COMPETITIVE GAMER

"You cannot be serious!" is the cry most often heard from Competitive Gamer's mouth, and the noise is swiftly followed by a series of crashes, bangs and wallops as items are thrown around the room in frustration. One cannot argue with a bossy little computer and win. So, the player must dedicate himself to the game, and like basketball star Kobe Bryant does with his free-throws, practice, practice, practice and practice some more. It doesn't matter whether it is sunny outside or "Battlestar Galactica" is on TV: Competitive Gamer is totally focused on beating the game.

GAMER TIMELINE

Ah, don't they grow up fast?

Forget that old height chart where you marked off Gamer's measurements in feet and inches. On the right, is the correct way to record a serious Gamer's progress through life:

The pearly gates of gaming heaven
Wii
DS Lite
XBOX 360
XBOX
PS3
PS2
PSx
PSOne
SEGA dreamcast
SEGA nomad
SEGA genesis
Sega CD
SEGA 32x
SEGA
NGC
N64
SNES
NES
ATARI 2600

PLOT IDOL

Gamer's favorite bedtime stories

It is all too easy for Gamer to accuse you of not knowing what you are talking about every time you criticize his gaming habit because, er, he's right. Fret no longer: peppered throughout this book you will find helpful explanations of plots for all his favorite games. Now you are free to rant whenever the mood takes you, safe in the knowledge that Gamer cannot shoot you down...

LEGO STAR WARS

Set in a galaxy far, far away, where no one raises an eyebrow at *Star Wars* faces painted on little Lego characters. Even the sceptical have to admit that Princess Leia's bagels-on-ears hairstyle lends itself particularly well to a Lego headband. The good vs. evil battle rages on, with the excitement of Jedis with Lightsabers causing palpitations in your Gamer. Your cat runs scared from the room as Chewbacca rips off arms, and red power bricks get thrown around like confetti at a particularly dangerous wedding. In the words of Yoda: "When Lego character you become, dignified rest there is not."

HALO

It is the future. Life, as you know it, is history. Sorry, it's too late now to start reusing plastic bags and composting potato peelings. What is left of Earth is threatened by an alien alliance hell-bent on death and destruction. Ouch. But there is a saviour: a cybernetically enhanced man, a soldier so bereft of humanity he could make a vampire weep garlicky tears. Hello, Master Chief. With the aid of a large and interesting array of weaponry he can save the world from the alien scum…

MADDEN NFL

Glory and riches await the chosen few who become professional football stars but there is hope for the average person, the two left-footed human being aka Gamer. If Gamer chooses his team wisely then glory beyond all gloriousness awaits. He can scale the heights of the semi-pros, and eventually soar to superstardom when he leads his team to Super Bowl victory. You might wonder why your hard-earned nickels and dimes are annually guzzled by a new version of *Madden*. Well, it's because the men in suits reproduce the same game every year, with carefully measured enhancements that suck the cash from your wallet and the free will from Gamer's mind in equal measures. And still, still we wait for the cheerleader application. *Madden*'s great rival, *Blitz: The League II*, should take advantage of that gap in the market.

WHAT NOT TO SAY
to a Gamer

It is just your luck that when Gamer finally puts down the console and cocks half an ear in your direction, the wrong thing will fly out of your mouth. He will then retrieve the console and throw himself into a gamer coma to save him from listening to you ever again.

So, be careful not to throw one of these conversational stink bombs into his ear space:

"Can I have a go? Which one am I?"

"I gave your console to the Police Athletic League. You don't mind, do you?"

"Turn that down, I've got a headache."

35

"YOU'RE NOT THE GRAND PRIX CHAMPION, YOU'RE JUST WEIRD."

"It's one in the morning. I am turning the game off."

"Are you listening to me?"

"IF YOU PUT THE SAME EFFORT INTO A PAPER AS YOU DID INTO THAT MACHINE, YOU'D BE A GRADE A STUDENT."

"So, about your report card..."

"IT'S YOUR TURN TO FEED THE CAT/TAKE OUT THE TRASH/GO TO THE SUPERMARKET."

"Hello, anybody home?"

"I'm sure you'd like the real world if you gave it a chance."

"I've decided to quit my job so we can all go and live in a tent and commune with nature."

GAMER STYLE & GROOMING

Gamer might not be living in the real world, but you are and you have to look at him.

Gamers catch a lot of flack for rejecting modern society's obsession with appearance. In many ways it is a good thing: they're never going to burn down the place with careless use of hair straighteners, for example. However, sometimes a gamer becomes too engrossed in gaming to remember to shower, which makes living with him less pleasant than it could be.

Use the following guide to help him with some basic style and grooming:

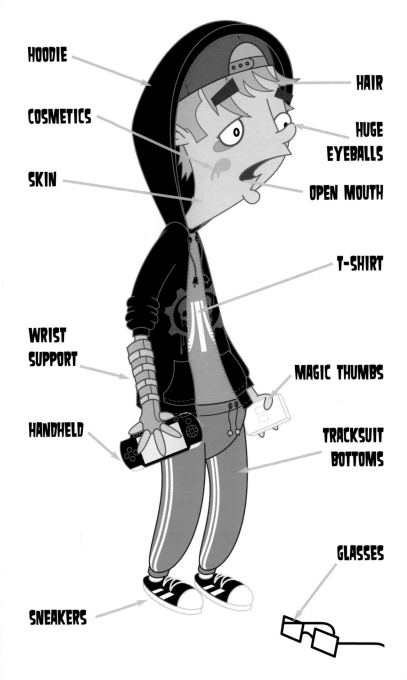

HOODIE

HAIR

COSMETICS

HUGE
EYEBALLS

SKIN

OPEN MOUTH

T-SHIRT

WRIST
SUPPORT

MAGIC THUMBS

HANDHELD

TRACKSUIT
BOTTOMS

GLASSES

SNEAKERS

Tracksuit bottoms **Look, he's changed out of his pajamas, so be grateful for that. Gamer wears his pants loose so he can sit down in them for 10-hour stretches without getting deep-vein thrombosis, or button marks embedded in his skin. The waistband has to be particularly forgiving so it can accommodate his engorged bladder—it is very hard to find a convenient moment to put down the console and go pee.**

T-shirt **He has a game-related T-shirt for every day of the week, and if you check your credit card statement you might notice he has taken the liberty of ordering one or two new ones online. Hmm. Still, at least he seems to have forgotten the fit he threw when you ironed the print on his tee into an unappealing mush.**

Hoodie **This beloved garment is not just for insulating Gamer against chill winds. Take a closer look at that hood: Is it not ideal for pulling over his head so he blocks out distractions from the game in his peripheral vision? He got the idea from watching a police horse wearing blinders and trotting calmly through a rowdy crowd. Gamer's eyes stay on the prize and no amount of arm waving while standing at his side will distract him.**

Sneakers **As one who has competed in the Grand Prix, the Super Bowl and several World Cups, albeit virtual ones, Gamer sees himself as a champion athlete. Therefore, he "needs" a fancy pair of sneakers, so do not try fooling him off with** cheap knock-offs bought at the discount shoe store or, of all places, the supermarket. Furthermore, anyone who points out his prized sneakers are redundant on his lazy, bedroom-bound feet will be pointedly ignored.

Hair Lank, yes; unwashed, all too often. It is quite deliberate though: having a freshly shampooed just-stepped-out-of-the-salon "do" on his head would mean smooth locks of hair bouncing into his face and putting him off the game. If the sour sight or fragrance of his hair gets to you, slap a baseball cap on his head. He won't make any best-dressed lists, but it will keep pesky, stray hairs out of his eyes.

Glasses He should fill his optical prescription but he chooses to shuffle closer and closer to the screen, instead. Constantly squinting at the monitor has burned his retina clean in two. The doc had never before seen such a case, and was genuinely impressed. Why aren't you!

Skin It is greyer than a grey squirrel in an old black and white film. Gamer does not care much for fresh air and physical exertion—at least, not when it is he who's doing it. You will only ever catch a flush in his cheeks when Gamer stands up too fast after beating the game and gets a massive head-rush.

Handheld Like Paris or Nicole with a luxe new handbag, Gamer is simply unable to put his handheld game down, even for a second. Has it become surgically attached to his hand?

Huge eyeballs **Gamer's peepers are so highly trained, he can spot enemies the nanosecond they drop into his peripheral vision. If he were in a real-life combat situation, he would be the only man to escape alive. As it is, he is only in a virtual combat situation, and nervously watching for zombies 24/7 is giving him red-eyed headaches. Make his day by bursting into the room and slapping a cold, soggy flannel on his eyes to ease the pain. If you can do this just as he breaks through to the final zombie stronghold, he's sure to be particularly appreciative. Don't worry if he shows this by shouting and banging his fists on the floor.**

Open mouth **When people die, their jaws lock tightly shut. When Gamer is worried he is about to die (on screen, of course), his jaw hangs low and lower, falling finally into a facial limbo. You find yourself strangely hypnotized by the elastic string of spit trailing from his open mouth but cannot find the words to point it out. You can't help but think that a bib would save him valuable laundry time.**

Cosmetics **Come again! Is this gamer guy really wearing make-up! But what else is that streak of orange across his face, if not some attempt at applying cheekbone-enhancing bronzer! Then you look a little closer, and realize that Gamer is, in fact, wearing a splash of curried noodle. It looks a bit crusty, as if it's been there a few days.**

Wrist support **Strangers might think this quiet, young fellow is only playing computer games because his wrist is in** a cast and he can't go out to play football with the other guys. Bless him. However, his medical records reveal that he is wearing a cast because of excessive gaming. Car manufacturers have crash test dummies to road-test their products; the makers of computer games have adolescent and teenage boys. You can almost hear the violins playing a sad tune for Gamer's lost youth. You need to find a lawyer to mount a class-action suit. Just don't tell the legal team quite how long Gamer plays, in case they start feeling sorry for the games manufacturer instead of him. You know what these lawyer types are like with their annoying moral stances.

Magic thumbs Even when Gamer isn't at the console, his thumbs are twitching. It occurs to you that his digits might be the pinnacle of evolution: they're not just opposable but seem to have actual minds of their own. One hundred years from now, Gamer's thumbs will be displayed in a jar of formaldehyde at the American Museum of Natural History. What a legacy.

8 REASONS TO RATE GAMER GIRLS

Stereotypically, gamers are boys. But the female of the species is deadlier than the male, and gamer girls exist in their gazillions.

This book often says just "he" for the sake of grammatical correctness. And because "he or she" takes a boringly long time to type. Sorry about that. Anyway, girls do, of course, play video games and kick ass. If you fail to understand the following list, she will probably do the same to you...

1 SHE HUSTLES LIKE A PRO

2 SHE UNDERSTANDS MALE PRIDE

3 SHE WASHES UP FINE

4 "NEEDY" IS NOT HER MIDDLE NAME

5 SHE IS MORE BIONIC WOMAN THAN BARBIE

6 IT TAKES MORE THAN A BROKEN NAIL TO MAKE HER CRY

7 SHE DOES NOT THINK IN PINK

8 SHE DOESN'T RELY ON GAMING FOR THE FASHION FORECAST

1 She hustles like a pro. **She has no moral dilemmas about practicing religiously in private then pretending she is new to the game. It makes wiping the floor with a guy gamer so much more satisfying, and never fails to entertain.**

2 She understands male pride. **If she is playing against a boy and his friends are watching, she is prepared to let him win if the bribe is sufficiently large. All the more money for new games the loser-boy can't afford.**

3 She washes up fine. **Just because she spends 90 percent of her waking hours gaming doesn't mean she looks barking mad in her online gaming profile photo. No, for that picture she has opted for flattering lighting and an expression somewhere between cute and I-will-eat-you-if-you-even-think-about-messing-with-me.**

4 'Needy' is not her middle name. **She has no truck with girls who whine about their boyfriends not paying enough attention to them. Her boyfriend can sympathize, though. He has an insatiable hunger for "quality time" and has signed them up for relationship counselling. You are advised against planning an engagement shower just now.**

She is more Bionic Woman than Barbie.
**Ahhh, flower fairies! Coooo, enchanted forests! Forget that.
All she really wants is a game where she rips opens the dark
heart of too-pink, too-fluffy, Barbie girly-ness in the "real"
world, and declares herself the new Queen.**

It takes more than a broken nail to make
her cry. **Shredded nails are worn with pride. Through
gaming, she has lost limbs and lives aplenty, and she didn't
cry about those, either. Besides, the shorter her talons, the
better her grip on the game.**

She does not think in pink. **When a game has
big, pink, patronizing writing on the front, she is tempted
to deface it with a marker pen. Frequently, she does, while
munching on a Snickers bar.**

She doesn't rely on gaming for the fashion
forecast. **She doesn't dress like Lara Croft in real life. Crop
tops are, like, so over. Hot-pants should never have been
invented. *Super Mario*-style dungarees do not look good on
anyone in real life.**

47

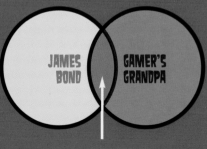

JAMES BOND

GAMER'S GRANDPA

GENTLEMAN GAMER

GAMER VENN: GENTLEMAN GAMER

The Gentleman Gamer has his grandfather's code of honor (no cheating, no crying, no giving up) combined with Bond's ability to walk away from a battle looking more than a little smug. Gentleman Gamer might appear to be generous and affable, but on no account will he let you win at his game. Well, not unless he can get away with trumping you by stealing your girlfriend and exposing your diamond-smuggling business. You have been warned.

WARNING!

A special note on game-related products:

There is nothing a savvy computer company won't do to squeeze another buck out of your Gamer.

PLOT IDOL II

More favorite bedtime stories

TOMB RAIDER

You are the daughter of a Lord with a small fortune at your disposal but no, that's not good enough for you. Something is missing. You're bored. In an attempt to rid yourself of this malaise you embark on a series of missions to seek hidden treasures in far-off lands, all while wearing amazingly skimpy shorts and impractical breast-tastic tops. Who would choose to wear overalls? Savage beasts, warlords and a seemingly endless amount of puzzles stand in your way but hey, you're Lara Croft. What else have you got to do!

CALL OF DUTY

You are at WAR! Grrr! Being the best of the best, you have been selected to go on a secret mission. Armed with your cunning and weaponry that would turn the Pentagon a bright shade of green, you must complete all the challenges that lie ahead. Don't get any ideas about personal glory though: this is all for the good of your country. Many lives depend on you as you slowly work your way closer to your glory and eventual victory. Anyone who interrupts you from this hugely important mission with distracting cries of "dinnertime!" should answer to the whole of humankind. So there!

POKÉMON

You are a pokémon trainer, longing to be the best trainer in the entire world. But others have the same idea. As you travel from competition to competition, you capture new pokémon and battle with other trainers for possession of their pokémon in duels. Each duel is fraught with danger, but knowing you will one day become the greatest trainer of all time helps you to eventual victory. Don't get complacent, though, because a new *Pokémon* game will be out next week and then you'll be back to the beginning again.

FAR CRY

You are Jack Carver, ex-Special Forces, and a man not to be messed with. But still there are fools who try ... They ambush your boat as you escort a journalist to a Micronesian desert island, threatening national security and—more important—your ego. You awake to find yourself in an inhospitable land but with one thought in your mind: Get that hot-looking journalist back and kill everyone in your way. Using stealth and, yep, you guessed it, a large array of weaponry, you conquer the forces of evil to rescue the reporter and put right what was wronged.

"NOW WE'RE GOING TO PLAY MY GAME"

The real world can be exciting, too!

Even if you manage to get a decent night's sleep with the myriad stresses of MRSA, bird flu, bluetongue, carbon emissions, melting ice and sinking jobs often hovering on the edge of your consciousness, there is more to worry about. Namely, how on earth are you going to connect Gamer to the real world?

Just as ex-cons are provided with support when they are released from prison, Gamer needs a period of adjustment to understand the non-gaming world. Basically, Gamer needs to learn how to play your game. This is how you can explain the rules of real life to him in a way he will understand:

"YOU CAN SCORE BONUS POINTS BY RETRIEVING THE CEREAL-ENCRUSTED BOWLS FROM UNDER YOUR BED."

Keep it simple: Gamer completes a task; Gamer gets rewarded with points. The best thing about this is that points are nothing more than an abstract concept. You don't have to pay for the return of your bowls—you can get away with saying, "Thanks, have 50 points," and Gamer will toddle off happily, looking for more stuff to give you back.

"IF YOU CLEAN MY CAR, YOUR LIFE WILL BE SPARED."

Classic time-pressure gaming here. As you set the clock, Gamer must grab a bucket and sponge and buff-away like crazy. If, at the end, you can't see your reflection in the hood, it's "Game Over," and the loser—NOT you—will be forced to leave the house and sleep in the garage. Not even the dog will bed down in there. The only confusion is that Gamer could argue that the game rules might dictate Gamer gets to keep the car he cleans and roar through town. Make it clear at the outset that things are different in this real-life game. The reward for winning at Clean-the-Car is that you get to sleep in a nice, warm bed.

"IF YOU MAKE A NOISE IN PROTEST AT GRANDMA'S SCRATCHY WHISKERS, YOU WILL EXPLODE!"

Fiendishly hard: Gamer must submit to a peck on the cheek from an elderly lady with a beard. Without saying a word. It will take all of Gamer's control to keep his Tourette's Syndrome in check, but the prize is great: if he can manage it, he will not be written out of her will.

"IN THIS GAME, YOU HAVE TO BE SUPERHUMANLY POLITE AND GENEROUS IN ORDER TO LIVE HARMONIOUSLY UNDER THE SAME ROOF AS US."

Appeal to Gamer's ambition to exhibit exceptional behavior, and you'll point the way to victory in this game. Every time you hear "please" or "thank you," throw in bonus points. When Gamer offers you the TV remote control, his score trebles. If Gamer is helpful in other ways: double points.

"TO REACH THE NEXT LEVEL, YOU MUST NEVER ASK FOR A LIFT WHEN I'M RELAXING. TO BECOME THE UNDISPUTED WINNER, DON'T EVEN THINK OF ASKING FOR THE CAR KEYS."

Allow Gamer any glorified title he likes for surrendering the annoying habit of asking—nay, demanding—to be driven over to his friend's house the moment you have kicked back, or are quite definitely not fit to get behind the wheel. Gamers gets bonus points for not using the phrases, "You're so unfair" or "Have you ever thought you have a drinking problem!"

GAMING IS DANGEROUS

It's not just zombies Gamer is scared of...

While Gamer dices with death on-screen, his body takes a beating in real life, too. Here are just a few of the medical ailments caused by gaming:

WII ARM

A very 21st-century condition, gained by prolonged and vigorous use of the Wiimote. Gamers' arms may get so sore, they take extended breaks from gaming. How interesting is that?

THUMB FREEZE

Waggling digits 24/7 sends them into a coma. The thumbs become so rigid, they're immobile. Though the afflicted gamer is stuck doing a permanent "thumbs-up," do not for a moment be fooled into thinking he is feeling cheerful.

EYE ACHE

Caused by forcing the eyes open well past bedtime. The exhausted eyeballs shrivel up and start burrowing back into the skull, desperate to find rest in a warm, dark place.

BACK STIFFNESS

The gamer might have a *Brain Training* age of 21, but a spine age of 89. Hello, Hunchback.

DEAD LEG

Gamer has had limbs blown clean off during war games, but nothing has hurt him as much as the tingling of a leg so asleep that it's practically dead. Encourage Gamer to jog up and down on the spot while continuing to play.

HEMORRHOIDS

A person can remain sitting for only so long without being bothered by hemorrhoids. It is rectal-examination o'clock. Sorry about that.

MADNESS

Eyes are closed but Gamer still SEES the game playing on, and he is powerless to prevent himself from dying. He shrieks in terror, flailing about like a frog in a food processor. It is up to you whether you call the men in white coats or just keep him quiet with another game.

GAMER

and the even bigger screen

To ease Gamer into a more socially acceptable screen-based hobby, sit him down in front of these classic films:

Juno	Juno How To Get To The End Of Level 5!
xXx	X@*x! Game Over
PS I Love You	PS I Beat You. Haaaa!
Highlander	Highscorer
The Devil Wears Prada	The Devil Wears Down My Fighting Strength
Dirty Dancing	Dirty Cheating
Anchorman	Skankyman In Yesterday's Clothes
Indiana Jones And The Last Crusade	Indiana Jones And The Last Game, I Promise
The Secret Adventures Of Tom Thumb	The Not-So-Secret Adventures Of My Thumbs
Kramer vs Kramer	Gamer vs Gamer

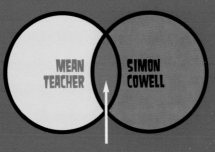

MEAN TEACHER SIMON COWELL

CONFIDENCE CRIPPLING GAMER

GAMER VENN: CONFIDENCE CRIPPLING GAMER

You might encounter the Confidence Crippling Gamer when you ask to have a turn on his console. "Pretty good for a first time, eh?" you say, feeling pretty pleased with yourself for not being killed off in the first 30 seconds. "In the words of Simon Cowell, 'You have just invented a new form of torture,'" replies Confidence Crippler. The last time tears stung your eyes like this was at school when your math teacher asked if you had a pooper-scoop bag for a brain. Ouch.

THE FOUR GREAT GAMER TRAPS

When young people dedicate their whole lives to gaming success, they risk running into a few problems along the way.

With this guide, you can help your resident gamer through...

TRAP #1:
Taking it too seriously

Gamer forgets that no one in the real world sees him as a seven-foot, muscle-covered, harem-owning warlord. He is so locked up in his gaming alter ego that he believes he is truly invincible. However tough the battle might get, he never breaks his legs, suffers a scar or even sheds a tear. You are concerned that when he finally encounters a small injury to his pride in real life, he will spend the rest of his years rocking and sobbing in a corner of his bedroom from the sheer shock of it.

Rescue operation

Challenge him to a game of real-life ping pong and show him who's boss. Where are his big guns now?

TRAP #2:
Speaking like a robot

Gamer has been known to say "lol" instead of actually laughing out loud. And he doesn't say "L-O-L" either: He actually says "lol." There is a school of thought that believes he should be arrested for his crimes against language and hung before dawn. This may sound a little draconian, but at least it might work—it's very hard to beg for your life in irritating text-speak.

Rescue operation

Send him to a Swiss finishing school, where he will not only learn correct grammar but also valuable life skills like standing up straight.

TRAP #3:
Losing his senses

Gamer-vision sets in after the 17th hour of play, whereupon the screen starts to float and Gamer is not sure whether his head is still neatly attached to his body. The room spins and he feels curiously dizzy. He sees stars at the peripheral edges of his vision. "Is this heaven?" he mumbles, but the words come out in a slurred mess, like a tramp who has been skulling home brew all day. Heaven isn't the home of nausea, he decides, before slumping down to the floor and pressing his hot, clammy cheek against the cool carpet.

Rescue operation

While he is dazed, move all the furniture in his room and nail it to the ceiling so that when he comes round, he will think he is floating. Far out, man.

TRAP #4:
Being paralyzed

Sitting in the same position for days at a time can turn a body to stone. So much energy has gone into keeping the thumbs moving that the rest of the body has shut down. The brain, though, whirs around in a panic. "Maybe this is part of the game?" the sufferer thinks, wondering if some mind-altering gas has seeped from the console into the surrounding air. When he realizes that it's impossible to move to check on whether a pulse remains, the shriek—not unlike that of a turkey on Thanksgiving Eve—can be heard in the next zip code.

Rescue operation

Strap the victim to an exercise floor mat and play sped-up Spice Girls on a loop until movement returns to the limbs.

THE GAMER
In Love

Please, let's get one thing straight: Gamers are not seriously attracted to video game characters. They're simply concerned that a relationship will rob valuable hours from their busy gaming schedules. Yet, the heart (or the hormones, more likely) is more powerful than the head and so Gamer will one day fall in love.

He or she doesn't even need to be in the same room as the object of desire, so don't expect a new face at breakfast. Romance can blossom online in a gaming forum—well, at least until the flirting between the two young lovers gets so cheesy that everyone else in the chatroom tells them to "get a thread."

Surprisingly, gaming has equipped them with the skills necessary for a successful relationship. They know, for example, how to push all the right buttons. Bound by the honor of true gaming, they do not cheat. Each is always up for a one-on-one and is quick to learn the best strategy for getting inside the other's base. They also understand the value of making an effort in order to secure a reward. For example, an acknowledgement of Valentine's Day can make sulkiness or jealousy disappear.

Lesser human beings run screaming from a relationship in stormy times. Gamers, however, never freeze up. If they hit a wall, they're not afraid to look online for recovery tips. A gamer learns from mistakes and is always keen to explore new content.

However, it has to be said that the guy gamer often already has a mistress who is nothing if not demanding. Gaming captured his heart first and he is not about to lower his scores for anyone. The strain of keeping up two passions is often more stressful for the male of the gaming species.

Love takes commitment to keep it firing on all cylinders. Gamers are well practiced at devotedly playing the same game for weeks, but when a game has been conquered, the player shops for a new one. Guys and dolls are much the same in this. Can a true Gamer be more committed to a relationship than the possibility of a fresh conquest? There is no easy answer. However, you can bet on one thing: Even a gamer in love is in no hurry to put the console into retirement...

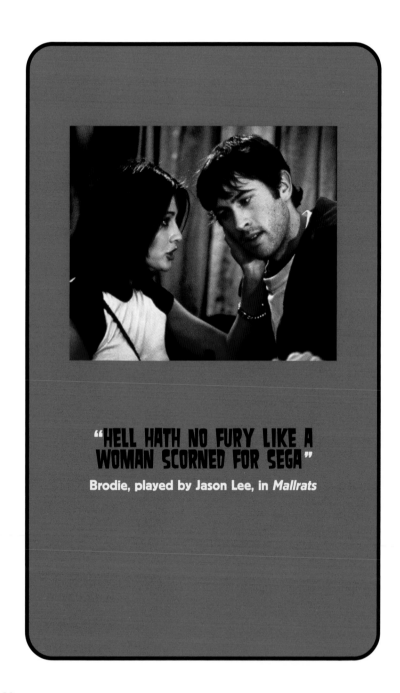

"HELL HATH NO FURY LIKE A WOMAN SCORNED FOR SEGA"

Brodie, played by Jason Lee, in *Mallrats*

HOW TO EMBARRASS
the Gamer

If he seriously wants anything like the success
he has on-screen in the real world, he needs
toughening up. In the future he will have
sleepless nights about paying the rent and will
worry endlessly about what to wear on Saturday
night. Cruel, cruel world. How can you help
prepare Gamer? Simple: give him a little bite
of the reality sandwich right now. He might even
get a taste for it.

STAGE 1:

As you enter his room, cough theatrically and don your
gas mask. Open the curtains, throw the window out wide
and spray him with Febreze. Does he even blush in
unwashed shame!

STAGE 2:

Email a round robin to your extended friends and family, with
news about what your household has been getting up to. Will
Gamer submit his latest *Super Mario* score to your newsletter?
Can he bear it that you refer to him by his online gaming
name to amuse your friends?

STAGE 3:

Before you pick him up from a party, paint *Gran Turismo* racing stripes down the side of your car and extend its exhaust pipe with toilet-paper rolls. Fill the back seat with speakers the size of shopping carts and play nothing but the sound of pumping exhausts and tires squealing on the road. Is he too ashamed to get in?

STAGE 4:

When he finally beats the game, rush outside ignite a firework display that spells "He's saved the world!" in the sky. Press champagne and canapés upon your bewildered neighbors. Is Gamer suddenly gripped with shyness and unable to come outside to hear the applause?

PARIS HILTON

MICHAEL JACKSON

ALL-THE-GEAR GAMER

GAMER VENN: ALL-THE-GEAR GAMER

Fortunately, Paris has sufficient millions to bankroll her passion for buying every designer garment that might ever be in fashion. Unfortunately for Michael Jackson, spending all your money on new gear while humming "Don't Stop Til You Get Enough" you'll be too broke to legally download him. All-The-Gear Gamer lies on the perilous middle ground between these two stars, spending every penny on games and gaming equipment. If you're related to Gamer, you may be reading this book in the Debtors Prison library. If you've still got your belt, my advice is to keep a firm grip on All-The-Gear Gamer's spending, or one of you will be locked up by Christmas.

PLOT IDOL III

And more favorite bedtime stories

GRAND THEFT AUTO

Forget saving the world. Let's not even pretend this is a noble cause. Money and crime are your only motivations as you roam the streets looking for your next victim or trick to pull. There are no limits as to how far you will rise in the crime world and nothing is too extreme as you steal, murder and pillage with little point, but with an aptitude not seen since *Tom and Jerry*. Your only real objective is to avoid the pesky cops and make as much money as you can before the next hood tries to take over your kingdom. Who could fail to be inspired by that?

GUITAR HERO

So long, console. You can now give your thumbs a well-earned break, so pick up the guitar and crank up the volume. You are the Grim Ripper, a rock star who looks frighteningly good in a pair of leather trousers (all things considered) and tickles his guitar into sweet submission. All you have to do is master the rhythm and keep the Rock Meter out of the red section—rather like keeping the groupies away from your mother. Rock on.

PROJECT GOTHAM RACING

You are a street racer, with little money but a knack for driving fast. So, you enter a few races and learn the hard way. After a while you earn enough to upgrade your car to a snazzy piece of machinery that puts your parents' old van to shame. Now you're winning, rising to the top. The races get tough, the opponents meaner but your winnings keep your car purring like the cheetah that got the cream. Soon you have no one left to race and you're the person everyone wants to beat. The phrase "quit while you're ahead" is not well known in these parts.

WORLD OF WARCRAFT

This is where it gets confusing, with MMORPGs. Come again! Massively multi-player online role-playing games, you nitwit. Call the games MMOs for short, and your Gamer will look at you in a new, respectful light. Basically, you create an avatar (a figure, like a Lego man but flashier) to represent yourself, then, by the power of the internet, you meet thousands of other players online in a digitally generated world. Some you collaborate with, some you kill—so it feels just like home. There are dungeons and trading, and with over 10 million subscribers it is busier than Walmart on a Saturday morning, if only the game could simulate endless lines and carts smashing into your undefended ankles. Nonetheless, it is apparently more addictive than the caffeine-laced candy aisle.

HAPPY BIRTHDAY,
Gamer!

**"Honestly, spending quality time with you is a gift
in itself—I don't need any more presents," is
a sentiment you will never hear as long as you
live with Gamer.** Presents are mandatory—
from any relative, pal or sap who lost the
roommate lottery and wound up with Gamer.
**Since technology does not come cheap, getting a
second job to help out Gamer is compulsory, too.**

Think back to all those times over the last year when
Gamer whined and begged for a new game or piece of
equipment, and you somehow kept his demands at bay
with the hope that he might get the goodies for his birthday.
Oh dear, that ruse is now ready to bite you on the bum.
Can you really deliver?

Of course you can't. Last year you spent an absurd amount of money on a game that the store clerk told you was very, very hard and Gamer finished it in three hours. This year, buy him something totally unexpected so he completely forgets about the long list of games and techie stuff he wants. (Have a look at the list on the right, then watch with joy as Gamer struggles to compose his best, "No really, you shouldn't have" face.)

BIRTHDAYS CALL FOR PARTIES.

Don't you want to do something special to celebrate!" you ask, as Gamer calls his usual gang over for a marathon session. He looks at you as if you are mad. Gaming with one's real friends is as special as it gets.

OK, you get it, you won't make a fuss. Maybe just some ice cream and cake, a mid-size bouncy castle and a clown who can do amazing things with balloon animals. It certainly creates an atmosphere. Gamer's friends fall around laughing (at the clown? At Gamer? At you?) but the birthday boy is keeping his head down. He is determined to ignore your presence and master the new game his friends pitched in for.

At least he's got one decent present.

PRESENT WISH-LIST*:

- Tambourine for his own version of *The Tambourine Hero*— that game is sure to take off.

- Front-row ticket to see *High School Musical on Ice*— everybody loves ice dancing.

- Bookstore gift certificate he's been dying to catch up with the National Book Award winners.

- Pair of roller blades they make him feel so free!

- Subscriptions to "*National Review*" and "*The Economist*"— so important for getting a jump on political debate.

*THE AUTHOR CANNOT ACCEPT RESPONSIBILITY FOR GAMER'S SATISFACTION WITH THESE GIFTS. DUHHH.

GAMER

On Vacation

Exploring the real world is not high on Gamer's list of priorities. For him, the sole purpose of vacation time off is to ramp up his gaming expertise. But seeing as there is absolutely no way you are prepared to leave him in the house alone for two whole weeks (Social Services can be so strict), Gamer is coming on vacation with you whether he likes it or not.

THE QUESTION OF WHETHER GAMER LIKES IT OR NOT DEPENDS GREATLY ON THE LOCATION OF YOUR GETAWAY.

He is keen to go to Toronto if his vacation time happens to coincide with the GX National Gaming portion of the Annual Fan Expo festivities. Otherwise, what's the point of leaving home?

You may have noticed that continued staring at the TV and computer screens have over-stimulated Gamer's senses. He would benefit from some time in a relaxing environment, you think, where he can enjoy the simple things in life and commune with nature. To that end, a week or two on a deserted tropical island would be character building. Gamer cannot play on his DS Lite because the blazing sun will make the screen go blank, so he will have nothing to do but listen to the gentle lap-lap of peaceful waves on the shore. If he can still remember how to read, bring a book for him to enjoy / throw at you, depending on his mood.

GAMER'S PACKING ESSENTIALS:

- Adaptor plug because his motto is "recharge, recharge, recharge"

- Earphones to shut out the world and enable him to really focus on the game

- DS Lite more essential than a passport

- Games library 50-odd games should do it. But allow space in the suitcase to buy new ones

- A note with his richest friends' and relatives' PIN numbers

Now the destination is settled and the tantrums have just about ceased, the next hurdle is getting him there. The airport is an issue for him, in that Gamer has experience of flying of his own accord, **simply by jumping on star-shaped objects and zooming off.**

If Gamer and the bundles of suspicious-looking wires in his bag do not come safely through the right side of airport security, don't give up. You have other vacation options. Camping in your car, for one. Or your backyard, depending on the season.

THAT WILL TEACH HIM. NO ELECTRICITY = NO GAMES.

Unless you count Monopoly? No, he does not.

Should his whining get too much for your frazzled nerves then pack him off to the nearest arcade with a fistful of quarters—did you really need them all for the laundry?—and you will be granted a whole day of peace. Or, for those with a tighter budget and a warped sense of humor, just open the nearest manhole. Gamer will dive in, *Sonic-The-Hedgehog*-style, before you can say, "I'm never going away with you again, you ungrateful sewer rat."

COMMUNICATION

Tips

Sometimes Gamer seems so lost in his computer world he can be hard to get through to.

Do you even understand what he is going on about half the time? Can he understand you? Does he know anything about the world on the other side of his screen? Try speaking his language to engage him in a deep and meaningful conversation:

"Ugh. Busy. Go away."

"To leave home as soon as possible."

"I wasn't joking."

"In that case, give me your credit card and let's see how happy I can be with plastic."

You despair. While Gamer finally sleeps in *Call Of Duty*-induced exhaustion, push hypnotist extraordinaire Paul McKenna into his bedroom and demand he does not leave until Gamer's mind has been bended away from its technological prison.

"Hello. My name is The Champion. I am your new adversary. My army will destroy you. Your Pokémons cannot save you now. I will be victorious!"

Ignores you and continues gaming → Return to beginning, repeat with another level of enthusiasm.

"As if. I will win and you will weep, big guy."

"Who are you?"

"Fair enough. Hey, I notice you've been gaming a lot recently – we haven't had a real conversation in weeks."

"It's only me! Had you fooled there for a moment, didn't I?"

"I've missed you something terrible. Let's talk."

"Why don't you just keep on talking to yourself and leave me out of it?"

"You're such a moron it's painful."

"Fantastic! How would you like a walk in the woods while we solve the problems of the world?"

"No way – what if someone from school sees me?"

"You're lucky I've got such a good sense of humor. I just wanted to see how you're doing – is there anything you need from me?"

No thanks. Why don't you just take me shopping so I can get that new game?"

"That sounds awesome. What shall we talk about?"

"For my ears to be surgically sealed shut so I won't be interrupted from my games ever again."

"I am not related to you. Please direct all questions to my agent."

"What do you want out of life?"

"Money is not the answer, my friend. Happiness cannot be built on dollar bills."

"About $200 should cover it. There's this new game and…"

"I don't understand. Your important function in life is to give me money. Cough up now."

"You are quite crazy."

"Devastated" does not even begin to describe it. You wander out of the house in a daze and awake to find yourself sitting in your car, getting beeped at by irate drivers as you fail to move at a green light, wondering where it all went wrong. Game Over.

THERE– DOESN'T BONDING FEEL GREAT?

PLOT IDOL IV

Yet more favorite bedtime stories

MARIO AND SONIC AT THE OLYMPIC GAMES

Imagine how proud you would feel to compete for your country in the Olympics. Then take a moment to consider how desperate you might feel if you were beaten to the finish line by a hedgehog. OK, so Sonic is a turbo-charged Speedy Gonzalez, but still: ouch. Your best bet is to train until you can leap over hurdles and throw the javelin in your sleep. You will even learn the art of skeet shooting and, um, cycling. Don't laugh: it's surprisingly difficult when you are Super Mario, because you are forever condemned to wearing dungarees instead of a nice spandex body suit, which would be far more aerodynamic.

FIFA STREET 3

There's no "i" in "team", but there is one in "FIFA". Forget the team: what have they ever done for you? You are a savvy street kid with a passion for soccer that will save you from taking a job where you ever have to get your hands dirty. This is gutter soccer, so it's all about tricks, style and flair, played in no-go areas in cities across the world. You are the undiscovered scoring genius, ready to show the world that soccer isn't a sport: at your feet, it is an art form. You turn your nose up at emerald green grass fields, preferring to skid around in the dramatic dust.

BRAIN TRAINING

You are an imbecile with the brain power of a potato; it is time to mash your grey cells into shape. At first you scoff at the simple addition and multiplication, but as the puzzles get fractionally harder, you have to unlock parts of your brain that have lain dormant since Mr. Oliver's math class. You discover that solving puzzles at "bicycle speed" will not earn you any carbon-neutral glory: if you are not working at "jet speed" and "rocket speed," you are nobody. As the days go past your scores start to improve, your memory sharpens and you start to feel the tingling of activity in areas of your skull that previously contained only dust. You develop an unhealthy dependency on Professor Kawashima and start to see his disembodied head bobbing around in your number-crunching dreams. You have never felt so mentally acute, but your friends will agree that you have never seemed such a boring blob.

MYSIMS

Let's face it—you are never going to find a spare half hour to clean the little patch of mold growing in your bathroom. However, you will find whole weekends to build furniture, houses and entire businesses as a Sim. You become obsessively interested in how to decorate your virtual home, despite the fact you are playing the game in a room so unkempt that pigs would refuse to set up a sty there. You find it very easy to overlook that fact. Don't tell your dorm mates you are too exhausted by doing tasks for members of the Sims community to put your dinner plate in the sink or the dishwasher. Just ignore them and play some more.

WHAT'S GOING ON...

... inside Gamer's Head?

It's just a matter of time before gaming becomes an Olympic sport—and I'm ready for the team. I need a new hoodie.

If I'm not mistaken, Lara Croft just gave me the eye. Hel-*lo*.

Why is the dog looking at me like he could do any better?

Die! Die! Yaaaaahhhh!

I just razed you with my laser-beam vision. Why are you *still* talking?

Blinking is *such* a waste of time.

I should film myself playing this thing because I am on fire!—pause—Is that the smoke alarm going off?

With my brute strength and razor-sharp cunning, I could be the next James Bond. The CIA is probably watching me pulverize this monster right now. Good evening, gentlemen.

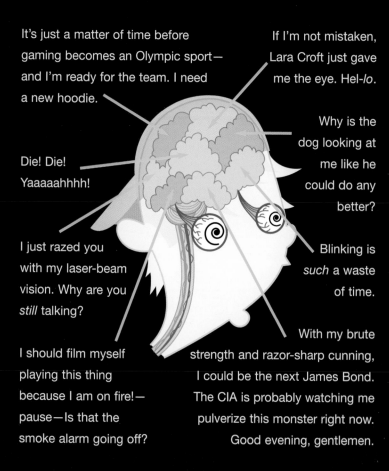

CHILD PRODIGY GAMER

GAMER VENN: CHILD PRODIGY GAMER

"Genius" is a dangerous word. Young people with talent are simultaneously gifted and burdened. At one end of the spectrum we have Britney Spears, the bright-eyed "Baby One More Time" star who got a little too involved with partying and went through psychiatric care, custody battles and self-styled baldness where the rest of us just experience a hangover. At the other end we have Mozart, the legendary child composer who worked himself into a very early grave. Does Child Prodigy Gamer stand a Lilliputian chance of being normal? You decide.

HOW TO COPE WITH GAMER'S

Moods

Being boggle-eyed and sleep-deprived does not help Gamer's sunny disposition. Gamer can be a moody little tyke sometimes. You blame *Sonic The Hedgehog,* **but Gamer and that game have become one and the same, faster than you can say, "Wii have a problem." Here's how to deal ...**

"Why are you being so unfair?" Take a moment. Is it worth making a stand against letting Gamer go to a gaming convention in Las Vegas without you—but *with* your credit card? Are you tough enough to hold your ground and stare down this one?

"No? No? Why not?" Ouch. Now you've gone and done it. Look at him: Right now Gamer's brow is furrowed in confusion, trying to work out why on earth he is unable to get what he wants. Do you know how much trouble you're inviting?

"I hate you! I hate you! I HATE YOU!"
Uh oh. Stand back. Not only does Gamer HATE YOU (does reading it a fourth time make it easier for you to bear?), this enthusiast has also slammed the console on the floor in a rage. You have an awful feeling that you are the one who will pay for that eventually. Sit on your hands to stop them trembling, and remember how thin your wallet is because if he starts crying, you know you are totally going to crumble.

"Don't you love me?"
A low blow. Is this how Gamer beats the living daylights out of all those games? And there you were, thinking Gamer's winning streak is due to superior thumb work and a few roundhouse kicks.

"I promise I will mow the lawn every weekend for a year."
This offer is unexpected. You have to run your hand through your hair and think about it. Then you shake yourself: No! You won't be bribed. You won't budge.

THE GAMER'S GANG

It is important you understand Gamer's social circle, because there are a few things that are very different about a gamer's friends.

They don't chitchat. **They don't chitchat.**
Communication is pared down to the most basic of signals—
thumb-waggles
on the console, foreign techie-talk and
whoops of "So CLOSE-ahhhh!"
Blowing the living doughnuts out of
your friends with a rocket launcher
is highly underrated, perhaps.
What these friends look like is
anyone's guess. All the
outsider can make out are
the backs of heads bent over
screens, surrounded by piles

of pizza crusts. **Do not think,**
however, that these pals are not
central pillars in the temple of
Gamer's happiness. When no
one else understands the
thrills of racing a pretend
pimped-up car, these
boys confirm to Gamer
that the endorphin rush
was, like, totally for real. He

is not imagining things.

They are not all there. **Not in the mental sense, you understand, but literally they are not all there. Some of Gamer's friends are at the other end of the country and even on the other side of the globe. No, Gamer has not been jet-setting on "borrowed" frequent-flyer miles:** Gamer met these folks on line. **Their idea of a good time is linking their computers together and fighting to the death.**

Gamer may refer to his friends as "party members" but that does not mean the residence you share is going to be trashed by party-mad gatecrashers. The party members are just all playing the same game. Singing from the same hymn sheet, sitting in the same sandbox.

If you would like to join the party, hijack Gamer's computer and message his online friends to introduce yourself. Bonding with the gang lounging in your house is tougher, but threatening to drive them back to their own housemates will ensure that they are nothing but friendly and polite to you from now on.

As you now know, Gamers are not introverted social outcasts. They are simply very selective, which makes the challenge of infiltrating their group all the sweeter.

THE GAMER

In the Future

Right now, Gamer cannot grasp this foreign concept, "growing up." Gamers imagine that they will forever be the same fun-loving kids, knowing how to have a good time. If only there wasn't the small question of paying the bills to contend with.

So, when he finally gets all the way to Level

30

what might be the right career path
for Gamer?

POLICEMAN

Because they traditionally wore white cotton gloves when directing traffic, just like *Sonic The Hedgehog*.

SOLDIER

War games have taught gamers all the military jargon they could ever need to know. However, they may be unprepared for all the community work the army does, like digging wells and repairing damaged old schools. "Where is my chopper?" the once and (we hope, future) gamer wails. "And why am I the only soldier here kitted out like Rambo?"

LIBRARIAN

"Books are a waste of time," Gamer says, keen to deter everyone else from using the library so he can sit at the computer in peace and game until closing time. He only took the job because the only library he'd ever heard of was full of games.

STUNTMAN

Gamer thinks he has an infinite supply of lives, so he has no fear of setting himself on fire and then rolling under a runaway train, only to be attacked by enemy snipers on the other side of the tracks.

FARMER

A childhood of stale indoors-y air means Gamer's lungs have a lot to catch up on. A job where he is out in the fields, day in, day out, is his only hope of ever shedding his deathly grey pallor. Plus, there are plenty of trees and cows to hide behind when he needs a *Brain Training* break on the handheld.

ACCOUNTANT

Gamer will get a kick out of using techie language that no one else understands. The temptation to spirit away other people's money and spend it on whizzy new games might bring about a hasty end to this career, though.

PERFORMANCE ARTIST

Gamer will take up residence at MOMA, sitting on a plinth as
he plays game after game after game. Museum-goers will take
photographs of his silvered face and marvel at the way he
does not notice anything else going on around him.

COULD I BE
A Gamer?

Living with a Gamer is tougher than conquering the final level of *Halo*.

But because you love him, you persevere, even deciding to play a game or two. It starts, of course, with *Brain Training*, the acceptable face of adult gaming. You stay up late to play, and sneak a guilty game in every time Gamer leaves the computer unattended. Then you shyly offer to take Gamer on, and, with your newfound dexterity and concentration levels, you whip ass. Pwned!